IN CASE OF EMERGENCY GUIDEBOOK

HOW TO FIND THE INFORMATION YOUR FAMILY NEEDS IF ANYTHING HAPPENS TO YOU

Maybe you've seen it with your friends or other family members: A sudden illness or accident leaves loved ones scrambling to track down information on medical conditions, financial accounts, keys to a lockbox, power of attorney documents, wills, and much more.

Failure to find this information can soon become a nightmare—especially if you're unable to tell loved ones where to go for the information they need to help you.

The In Case of Emergency Guidebook helps give your family these crucial details just when they may need them most.

Feel free to complete the entire Guidebook ... or even only a portion. Many people approach it by filling out the information they know off the top of their head right away. Then they add in pertinent details as they receive statements or other paperwork.

But regardless of your approach—your loved ones will probably agree that ANY information will be a big help when it comes to an emergency.

Important note: Please be sure to store this Guidebook in a secure place and inform a designated person of its location.

INDEX

Date completed/updated:

PERSONAL INFORMATION

Your name: ______________________________

Date of birth: ____/____/_________ Soc. Sec. #: ________________

Spouse's name: ______________________________

Date of birth: ____/____/_________ Soc. Sec. #: ________________

Living: ☐ Yes ☐ No If "no," date of death: ___/___/___________

Current address: ______________________________

Your phone: ______________________________

____

____

Spouse's phone: ______________________________

____

____

FAMILY INFORMATION

Number of Children: ________________

Number of living Children: ________________

CHILD #1:

Name: ____

Date of birth: ____/____/_________

Address: ____

Phone: _______________________

Spouse's name: ____

Spouse's Phone: _______________________________________

Names of grandchildren: _________________________________

____

CHILD #2:

Name: ____

Date of birth: ____/____/_________

Address: ____

Phone: _______________________

Spouse's name: ____

Spouse's Phone: _______________________________________

Names of grandchildren: _________________________________

____

CHILD #3:

Name: ____

Date of birth: ____/____/_________

Address: ____

Phone: _______________________

Spouse's name: ____

Spouse's Phone: _______________________________________

Names of grandchildren: _________________________________

____

CHILD #4:

Name: ____

Date of birth: ____/____/_________

Address: ____

Phone: _______________________

Spouse's name: ____

Spouse's Phone: _______________________________________

Names of grandchildren: _________________________________

____

CHILD #5:

Name: ____

Date of birth: ____/____/________

Address: ____

Phone: ______________________

Spouse's name: _______________________________________

Spouse's Phone: ______________________________________

Names of grandchildren: _______________________________

____

Notes: ____

____

____

____

____

____

____

____

____

____

PASSWORDS

Your personal cell phone: ______________________________

Your desktop computer: ______________________________

Your laptop computer: ______________________________

Your iPad or tablet: ______________________________

Email 1: ______________________________

Email 2: ______________________________

Other: ______________________________

Other: ______________________________

Other: ______________________________

Other: ______________________________

Other: ______________________________

Other: ______________________________

Do you keep a list of usernames and passwords for online accounts? .... ☐ Yes ☐ No

If "yes," where is the list located? ______________________________

____

Notes: ______________________________

____

____

____

____

MEDICAL INFORMATION

	Your	Your spouse
Have you assigned a medical Power of Attorney?	☐ Yes ☐ No	☐ Yes ☐ No

If "yes," who is it? ____________________

Location of document: ____________________

Do you have a living will?	☐ Yes ☐ No	☐ Yes ☐ No

Location of document: ____________________

Do you have a "do not resuscitate" (DNR) document?	☐ Yes ☐ No	☐ Yes ☐ No

Location of document: ____________________

Are you an organ donor?	☐ Yes ☐ No	☐ Yes ☐ No
Do you have known allergies?	☐ Yes ☐ No	☐ Yes ☐ No

If "yes," please list: ____________________

____

Do you have diagnosed medical conditions?	☐ Yes ☐ No	☐ Yes ☐ No

If "yes," please list: ____________________

____

Do you currently take any medications?	☐ Yes ☐ No	☐ Yes ☐ No

If "yes," please complete the medication card contained in the back of this Guidebook.

DOCTOR INFORMATION

Name of your primary doctor: ____________________

Your doctor's address: ____________________

Your doctor's Phone: ____________________

Name of spouse's primary doctor: ____________________

Spouse's doctor's address: ____________________

Spouse's doctor's Phone: ____________________

Name of your dentist: ____________________

Your dentist's address: ____________________

Your dentist's Phone: ____________________

Name of spouse's dentist: ____________________

Spouse's dentist's address: ____________________

Spouse's dentist's Phone: ____________________

	Your	Your spouse
Do you see other doctors?	☐ Yes ☐ No	☐ Yes ☐ No

If "yes," please list below:

DOCTOR #1:

☐ You ☐ Your spouse

Doctor's name: ____________________

Specialty: ____________________

Address: ____________________

Phone: ____________________

DOCTOR #2:

☐ You ☐ Your spouse

Doctor's name: ______________________

Specialty: ______________________

Address: ______________________

Phone: ______________

DOCTOR #3:

☐ You ☐ Your spouse

Doctor's name: ______________________

Specialty: ______________________

Address: ______________________

Phone: ______________

DOCTOR #4:

☐ You ☐ Your spouse

Doctor's name: ______________________

Specialty: ______________________

Address: ______________________

Phone: ______________

PHARMACY INFORMATION

Pharmacy's name: ______________________

Address: ______________________

Phone: ______________

Notes: ____

INSURANCE INFORMATION

HEALTH INSURANCE

Your health insurance:

☐ Private ☐ Employer-sponsored ☐ Medicare

☐ Medicare supplement ☐ Medicaid

Issuing company: ______________________________

Policy owner: ______________________________

Policy #: ______________________________

Agent: ______________________________

Do you have separate
prescription drug coverage? .... ☐ Yes ☐ No

If "yes," please answer below:

Issuing company: ______________________________

Policy owner: ______________________________

Policy #: ______________________________

Agent: ______________________________

Your spouse's health insurance:

☐ Private ☐ Employer-sponsored ☐ Medicare

☐ Medicare supplement ☐ Medicaid

Issuing company: ______________________________

Policy owner: ______________________________

Policy #: ______________________________

Agent: ______________________________

Do your spouse's separate
prescription drug coverage? .... ☐ Yes ☐ No

If "yes," please answer below:

Issuing company: ______________________________

Policy owner: ______________________________

Policy #: ______________________________

Agent: ______________________________

HOMEOWNERS OR RENTERS INSURANCE

Issuing company: ______________________________

Policy owner: ______________________________

Policy #: ______________________________

Agent: ______________________________

AUTO INSURANCE

Issuing company: ______________________________

Policy owner: ______________________________

Policy #: ______________________________

Agent: ______________________________

LIFE INSURANCE

PLAN 1

Type: ☐ Term ☐ Whole ☐ Variable

☐ Universal ☐ Final Expense

Issuing company: ______________________________

Policy owner: ______________________________

Policy #: ______________________________

Agent: ______________________________

PLAN 2

Type: ☐ Term ☐ Whole ☐ Variable

☐ Universal ☐ Final Expense

Issuing company: ______________________________

Policy owner: ______________________________

Policy #: ______________________________

Agent: ______________________________

PLAN 3

Type: ☐ Term ☐ Whole ☐ Variable

☐ Universal ☐ Final Expense

Issuing company: ______________________________

Policy owner: ______________________________

Policy #: ______________________________

Agent: ______________________________

PLAN 4

Type: ☐ Term ☐ Whole ☐ Variable

☐ Universal ☐ Final Expense

Issuing company: ______________________________

Policy owner: ______________________________

Policy #: ______________________________

Agent: ______________________________

LONG-TERM CARE INSURANCE

PLAN 1

Issuing company: ______________________________

Policy owner: ______________________________

Policy #: ______________________________

Agent: ______________________________

PLAN 2

Issuing company: ______________________________

Policy owner: ______________________________

Policy #: ______________________________

Agent: ______________________________

OTHER INSURANCE COVERAGE

PLAN 1

Type of insurance: ______________________________

Issuing company: ______________________________

Policy owner: ______________________________

Policy #: ______________________________

Agent: ______________________________

PLAN 2

Type of insurance: ______________________________

Issuing company: ______________________________

Policy owner: ______________________________

Policy #: ______________________________

Agent: ______________________________

PLAN 3

Type of insurance: ______________________________

Issuing company: ______________________________

Policy owner: ______________________________

Policy #: ______________________________

Agent: ______________________________

PLAN 4

Type of insurance: ____________________________________

Issuing company: ____________________________________

Policy owner: ____________________________________

Policy #: ____________________________________

Agent: ____________________________________

Notes: ____________________________________

____

____

____

____

____

____

____

____

____

____

____

____

FINANCIAL INFORMATION

Do you have a financial professional? .... ☐ Yes ☐ No

Financial professional's name: ____________________

Firm's name: ____________________

Address: ____________________

Phone: ____________________

Have you assigned Financial Power of Attorney? .... ☐ Yes ☐ No

If "yes," who is it? ____________________

Location of document: ____________________

Do you have a safe deposit box? .... ☐ Yes ☐ No

Location of box: ____________________

Box #: ____________________

Location of key: ____________________

NON-INTEREST-BEARING BANK ACCOUNTS

(Ex. Cash account, checking account)

ACCOUNT 1

Type: ____________________

Bank name: ____________________

Account owner: ____________________

ACCOUNT 2

Type: ______________________________

Bank name: ______________________________

Account owner: ______________________________

ACCOUNT 3

Type: ______________________________

Bank name: ______________________________

Account owner: ______________________________

ACCOUNT 4

Type: ______________________________

Bank name: ______________________________

Account owner: ______________________________

INTEREST-BEARING BANK ACCOUNTS

(Ex. savings account, certificates of deposit (CDs), money market account)

ACCOUNT 1

Type: ______________________________

Bank name: ______________________________

Account owner: ______________________________

ACCOUNT 2

Type: ______________________________

Bank name: ______________________________

Account owner: ______________________________

ACCOUNT 3

Type: ______________________________

Bank name: ______________________________

Account owner: ______________________________

ACCOUNT 4

Type: ______________________________

Bank name: ______________________________

Account owner: ______________________________

TAX-ADVANTAGED SAVINGS ACCOUNTS

(Ex. IRAS, SEPs, pensions, 401(k), annuities, other qualified savings accounts)

ACCOUNT 1

Type: ______________________________

Financial institution: ______________________________

Account owner: ______________________________

ACCOUNT 2

Type: ______________________________

Financial institution: ______________________________

Account owner: ______________________________

ACCOUNT 3

Type: ______________________________

Financial institution: ______________________________

Account owner: ______________________________

ACCOUNT 4

Type: ______________________________

Financial institution: ______________________________

Account owner: ______________________________

STOCK, BONDS, AND MUTUAL FUNDS

ACCOUNT 1

Type: ______________________________

Financial institution: ______________________________

Account owner: ______________________________

ACCOUNT 2

Type: ______________________________

Financial institution: ______________________________

Account owner: ______________________________

ACCOUNT 3

Type: ______________________________

Financial institution: ______________________________

Account owner: ______________________________

ACCOUNT 4

Type: ______________________________

Financial institution: ______________________________

Account owner: ______________________________

HOME AND VEHICLE

Do you own your home or rent? .... ☐ Yes ☐ No

If you own your home, how are property taxes paid?

☐ You pay them ☐ They're handled through your mortgage

Do you have a mortgage? .... ☐ Yes ☐ No

Mortgage institution: ______________________________

How is the mortgage paid?

☐ Check mailed ☐ Online payment
☐ Automatic payment each month

Do you have a home equity loan or
home equity line of credit? .... ☐ Yes ☐ No

LOAN 1

Type: ☐ Home equity loan ☐ Home equity line of credit

Mortgage institution: ______________________________

How is the loan paid?
☐ Check mailed ☐ Online payment
☐ Automatic payment each month

LOAN 2

Type: ☐ Home equity loan ☐ Home equity line of credit

Mortgage institution: ______________________________

How is the loan paid?
☐ Check mailed ☐ Online payment
☐ Automatic payment each month

CAR LOAN 1

Financial institution: ______________________________

How is the loan paid?
☐ Check mailed ☐ Online payment
☐ Automatic payment each month

CAR LOAN 2

Financial institution: ______________________________

How is the loan paid?
☐ Check mailed ☐ Online payment
☐ Automatic payment each month

CREDIT CARDS/DEBIT CARDS

CARD 1

Type: ☐ Credit card ☐ Debit card

Account holder: ______________________________

Financial institution: ______________________________

CARD 2

Type: ☐ Credit card ☐ Debit card

Account holder: ______________________________

Financial institution: ______________________________

CARD 3

Type: ☐ Credit card ☐ Debit card

Account holder: ______________________________

Financial institution: ______________________________

CARD 4

Type: ☐ Credit card ☐ Debit card

Account holder: ______________________________

Financial institution: ______________________________

TAX INFORMATION

Do you have an accountant? .... ☐ Yes ☐ No

Accountant's name: ______________________________

Firm's name: ______________________________

Address: ______________________________

Phone: ______________

Location of past tax returns: ______________________________

____

MILITARY SERVICE

Branch of service:

☐ Army ☐ Navy ☐ Air Force ☐ Marines

☐ Coast Guard ☐ USPHS ☐ Other: ______________

Service #: ______________________________

Date of entry into active duty: ______/______/__________

Date of separation: ______/______/__________

Place of separation: ______________________________

Location of certified discharge papers: ______________________________

____

IMPORTANT DOCUMENTS

Will .... ☐ You ☐ Your spouse

Location of will: ______________________________

____

Do you have a trust? .... ☐ Yes ☐ No

Type: ☐ Living ☐ Testamentary ☐ Revocable ☐ Irrevocable

Attorney of financial professional who set it up: ______________

Trust name: ______________________________

Location of documents: ______________________________

Current passport .... ☐ You ☐ Your spouse

Location of Passport: ______________________________

____

Social Security card .... ☐ You ☐ Your spouse

Location of Social Security cards: ______________________

____

Marriage certificate .... ☐ Yes ☐ No

Location of marriage certificate: ______________________

____

Birth certificate .... ☐ You ☐ Your spouse

Location of birth certificate: ______________________________

____

Death certificate .... ☐ You ☐ Your spouse

Location of birth certificate: ______________________________

____

Vehicle titles .... ☐ Yes ☐ No

Location of titles: _______________________________________

____

Divorce decrees .... ☐ Yes ☐ No

Location of divorce titles: _________________________________

____

FINAL WISHES

Would you prefer to be:

☐ Buried ☐ Cremated ☐ Other: ______________________

Would your spouse prefer to be:

☐ Buried ☐ Cremated ☐ Other: ______________________

If you prefer burial, have you purchased
a plot in a cemetery? .... ☐ Yes ☐ No

If "yes," please complete:
Cemetery name: ______________________________

Address: ______________________________

Phone: ______________________

Have you already made pre-paid
arrangements with a funeral home? .... ☐ Yes ☐ No

If "yes," please complete:
Funeral home name: ______________________________

Address: ______________________________

Phone: ______________________

Please share any preferences you may have regarding a funeral, celebration of life, pallbearers, officiant, or other final wishes:

____

____

____

____

____

____

____

____

____

____

CURRENT MEDICATION LIST

Name: ______________________________

Last update: ______________________________

Medicine	Dosage	Frequency	Doctor

CURRENT MEDICATION LIST

Name: ______________________________

Last update: ______________________________

Medicine	Dosage	Frequency	Doctor

CURRENT MEDICATION LIST

Name: ______________________________

Last update: ______________________________

Medicine	Dosage	Frequency	Doctor

Notes:

Notes: ______________________________

Notes:

Notes:

Notes: ____

Notes:

Notes:

Notes:

Notes:

Notes:

Notes: ____

Notes:

Notes:

Notes: ____

Notes:

Notes:

Notes: ____

Notes:

Notes: ____

Notes: ____

Notes:

Notes:

Notes:

Notes:

Notes:

Notes:

Notes:

Notes:

Notes:

Notes:

Notes:

Notes:

Notes:

Notes:

Notes: ____

Notes:

Notes:

Notes:

Notes:

Notes:

Notes: ____

Notes:

Notes:

Notes:

Notes:

Notes:

Notes:

Made in the USA
Monee, IL
04 November 2026

67386131R10046